CW00666717

Guernsey

A little souvenir

CHRIS ANDREWS

Saints Bay

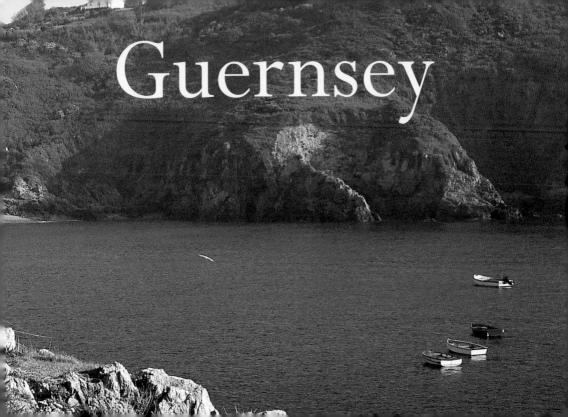

Guernsey

The second largest of the Channel Islands, Guernsey sits proudly in the Gulf of St. Malo in the Bay of Normandy. Described by Victor Hugo as "Fragments of France which fell into the sea and were picked up by England", the feeling this mixed parentage brings is unique, a mingling of relaxed Gallic insouciance and a sense of British orderliness creates an identity distinct from any other.

Originally part of the European land mass – high hills set above plains – the Channel Islands are now in the unique position of being close enough to France to see it, but part of the British Isles. The Bailiwick of Guernsey was originally part of the Duchy of Normandy. This changed in 1066 when Duke William of Normandy became King William I (William the Conqueror) of England, defeating King Harold at the Battle of Hastings. Hence today some Islanders argue that the British Isles are owned by Guernsey, not vice versa!

There are ten parishes in Guernsey: St. Peter Port, St. Sampson, Vale, Câtel, St. Andrews, St. Saviour, St. Martin, Forest, Torteval and St. Pierre du Bois. Each parish is represented in the States by a number of elected independent Deputies, and they each have a council, called a

6 L'Ancresse

Douzaine, who are responsible for more parochial matters such as collecting rates and the bi-annual inspection of streams and hedges. Alongside its own government, Guernsey has its own banknotes, postal system, and its own language. Guernsey patois, Guernesiaise, is a language based on Normandy French of some 900 years ago; it was the official language of the Island until 1921 when it was superseded by English. "Sarnia" as Guernsey is known in the local patois, translates as "Green Land". Although now heavily built up in some areas, there are still many places of natural beauty. The South Coast, stretching from Pleinmont to Jerbourg, boasts soaring cliffs and green headlands punctuated by small, sheltered coves.

Local produce at the West Show 7

Sunset at Cobo Bay

The landscape of the West Coast is lower and gentler, bays are more open here and often feature large rock formations. The beaches on this side of the Island are renowned for their good surfing, and occasionally at very low tides the remains of an ancient forest can be seen breaching the sands of Vazon Bay. L'Ancresse and Pembroke Bays dominate the North Coast, sweeping across it with their wide expanses of pale sand. Inland there are historic buildings, rural landscapes and working farms with livestock.

10 The south coast

Vazon Bay 11

12   Moulin Huet Bay and The Pea Stacks (rocks at the end of the point)

Cobo and Vale at dawn   13

14   Vazon Bay with Fort Hommet and Albecq to the left

Saints Bay and the south coast from the cliff path   15

16 The south coast and St Martin's point

An old store above Petit Bot and sea and rock at Portinfer 17

18 View east from Le Gouffre

Sunset looking west from Les Tielles   19

20 St Martin's Point at the south east

The north east coast, Portinfer to Grande Havre 21

22 Sunset at Cobo, looking out to sea

Choppy sea round rocks looking into Cobo Bay

North over Cobo to Saline Bay

26   Icart Point from the cliff path at Petit Bot

The QEII at anchor in the Little Russell between Guernsey and Herm   27

28 St Peter Port, the Town Marina and the Albert Pier

Classic boats moored in the Town Marina   29

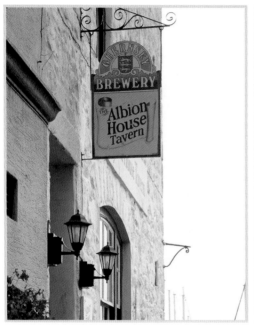

30   Local pubs with the local brew

32   Smith Street leading to the High Street

Yachts and floral show on the Quayside 33

34   Irises and one of the gardens at Castle Cornet

The Harbour front at night   35

36   Centre of the Town from Fort George

38   Fishing from the Castle Cornet breakwater and...

The Town Marina and Castle Cornet with St Sampsons beyond

42   Rooftops in St Peter Port

Christmas lights in Town   43

44   Government House and Victor Hugo's House

46   Greenhouse flowers

48   Spring in St Peter's

50   A stone store showing some signs of age

Dahlias in a Guernsey farmhouse garden

52   Cultivated flowers in Candie Gardens

Wild cliff flowers at Les Tielles   53

54   L'Ancresse and Pembroke at the north of the Island

St Peter Port Harbour at dawn

58   Rocquaine Bay and Fort Grey at low tide

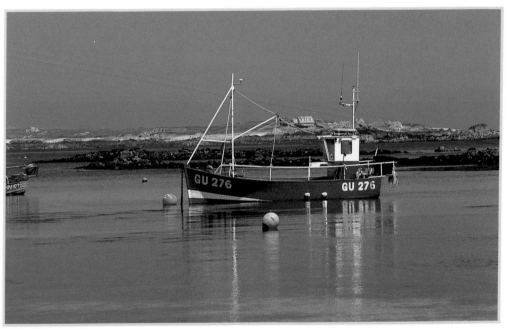

Moorings at Portelet with Lihou beyond   59

60   Noire Pute with the QEII in the distance

62   The violence of a winter storm at Vazon bay

A quiet spring dawn at Rocquaine 63

First published 2005

Reprinted 2006, 2011

Photographed and produced by Chris Andrews Publications Ltd
15 Curtis Yard, North Hinksey Lane, Oxford, OX2 0LX

Tel: +44(0)1865 723404 email: enquiries@cap-ox.com

www: cap-ox.com

Text: Dallas Masterton

ISBN 978 1 905385 00 3

Front Cover: St Peter Port Harbour and The Town
Back Cover: Candie Gardens
Title Page: Guernsey Wild Orchids